our floral anatomy

Ashlin Artemesia

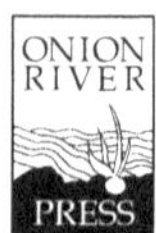

Onion River Press
191 Bank Street
Burlington, VT 05401

ISBN: 978-1-949066-80-7

for gardens

Illustrators, Editors and Artists

Olakiitan Adeola
Violet Antonick (p 24, 52)
Julia Blasius (p 30, 42)
Gemma Cirignano (p 20, 22, 32)
Angelica Fuentes
Jen Hao
Katherine Lazarus
Isadora Marks
L & G

to many more, thank you for the water

[intro]

a cassette tape and flower pot, this collection reads as a series of dancing, stinging anecdotes and memories

in the process of thriving towards light, I am aware of you, reader, who may be singing along, bathing in water, or listening as a soundtrack of heartbeats collected

tape enters the player, rewind

malnourishment

press play

we could have used the rain we made
your tension rising…

drowned in our sky I could not find those stars we loved buried beneath
impoverished despair of the air this night, oxygen a burdened weight, a
friend extinct in azure I remember they disappeared I remember night
glassy/sky milky as this faucet of stars sprinkled as blinding as your eyes

i.
though I had no shield my iron sheath withdrew you pulled it out of me a
sword between my feet the same sword you used to pierce that sensitive
bundle of blood that simmering stem on edge and then I grew, I grew till my
split ends hit the ceiling a convergence of energies melting as one you
sautered me

ii.
my memory is of lying flat on the ground my protruding knee the only
mountain that surfaced from the battle of love the battle like an idiosyncratic
replay of a song you deemed fit only you could declare only you had control
as I was not obsessed with the matter I did not make that my being my reason
for breath you pushed this mountain up and over carpets I think the lamp
shattered the tumbling was not normal but you said it so, the shoving the bar
fight you created, the simulation you placed within us

iii.

crazed eyes fell on me and as those curtains drew I knew the playlist was
complete the bruises were tiny but that was only the shell, the internal was
crushed a set of combusting engines were my bones it rang SO loud SO loud
the fire eating inside my ears but what music to you what sweet instruments
play

iiii.

the worst was the tenderness in accomplice with sick murder of entrails how
dare you combine comfort and slaughter how dare you suffocate my alarm
how dare you wrap your hands around the most delicate canal of air out of
pure self-hatred a tactic enacted as deflection no longer used while pleasuring
me *there is no me* there is only a mirror and that mirror reflects the guilty party
the case has closed there is no jail time there is an unsafe system and I have
shut the doors

press stop

mutual butterflies

we contemplate the wings on things

why did you want to fly?
I like it here, on the ground, next to your shadow
while most cool
yours is a warm home

you knew I prefer to float in cloudless oceans

our souls swim to sea
breath by breath
drinking our way to the other's side

how desperate my heart is
to sink into
to be your puddle

[fast forward]

we walked on the dock that evening
it was August, the wind had balmy rage
I was trying to match your feet's speed
you liked me stuck in the corner of your eye, running behind

boats lined in a row bobbled
they answered the water welling in my eyes, they wavered yes and
keep running but
wrong direction

my favorite kind of air I felt lucky to breathe
all the mist we couldn't see
a fight between us broke,
now you were catching up to me

determined I wanted to disappear into the sky

the first time I wanted to fly

13

med
honey

it is not enough

in me,
the turbulent water of dreams
my creative calls
begs to pour out
sugar-crusted crystals
my metamorphosis occurring

life leaking out my limbs

the sunshine gives

I kiss goodbye time,
that star stitched in my veins
is strong
scintillating
fissures   on   nerves

he cracked me open

ah,
there

boiling point

only the waterfall ensues:

*he burnt the petals he grew
a match so convincing*

*spells on his pupils
are more than red flags*

addiction
is leman

I sketch an outline of my palms,
a language you wrote onto me
profound and just

I spilled
my tongue
over
you

the fraction you gave,
it is not enough

the tea I drank,
you, Med

you glaciate:

I rain

your sound

I've learned all I can from you
smudging the sides of my brain like butter

sometimes I check the weather
to see if we're sharing rain

preserving our memories is
holding onto a peach pit

your toffee cradled itself deep into my molars
one lick and there's treacle
soaked teeth

I cannot drill you out
pit buried and flamed

no surprise
when the peach tree arrives
lifeless
soil defunct

I still find cavities

it was our joke, that I bruise like a peach,
from teeth
from harsh handling
I liked it
the meal, the feast

these brandings were remnants of my dessert
juice of a peach reminds me
the sugar fades
the pit cracks bone if your bite is too brittle

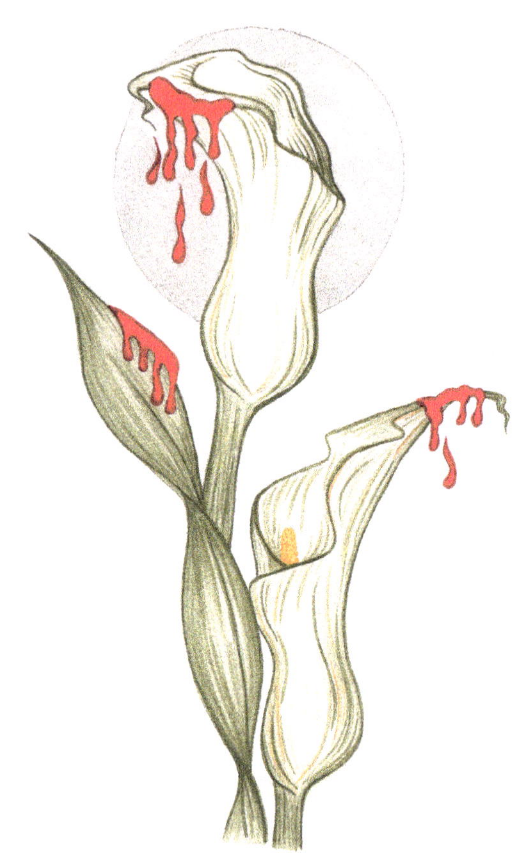

morphology

i.

    I believe growth is our floral anatomy
    firm roots hold tight against a ruckus of waves

    share moon
    share sun
    share drinks on our leaves
    share pots of soil we dance in

    independent blossom, in delights of murky seasons
    how delicate we bloom
    how vulnerable we open
    exposed veins become less and less timid

    share moon share sun   share moon share sun

    the spikes on our elbows are indeed jarring
    even if our scent is luring

ii.

    on empath maps,
     roads less traveled

    how you feel, this is charted
    territories unknown
    best distinguished when flowering

when time becomes a limb, it is invested in your blood flow
        flow
            flow
              flow
                flower

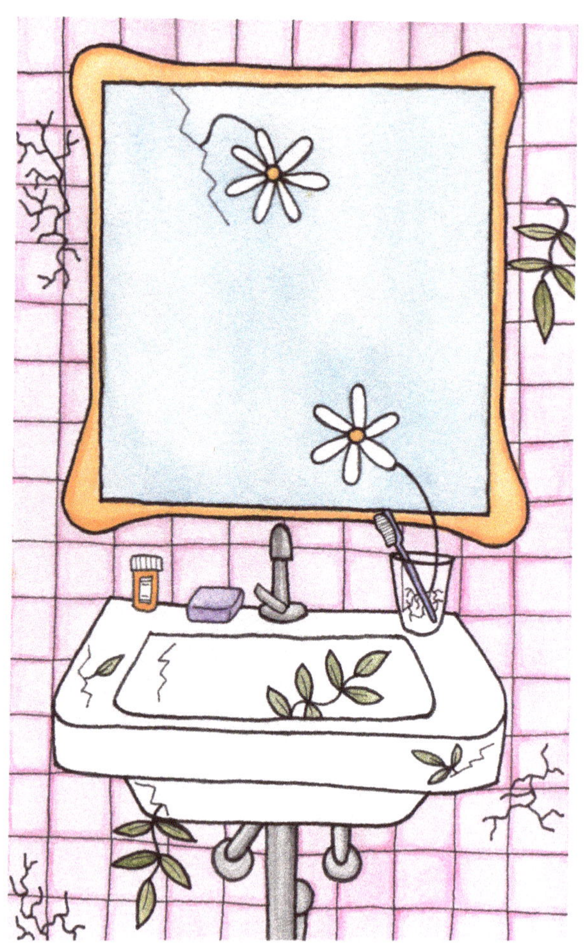

dance again

i.

learning to breathe, manifesting my oxygen

in sidewalk's crevices
your roots are weak

mine grow thick and inviolable,
friends between cement and wood

I found
unboundedness
resilience

forgiveness became prescription

ii.

someday someone will drink me
my glass is now quarter full,
I had put it near the sink for you

in hibernation, hanging my petals on setting sun's shoulders
allowing roots to stretch, unclench, detangle
mustering all might [this comes with creating your own elements]

learning to swim to breathe again
learning to breathe to swim again

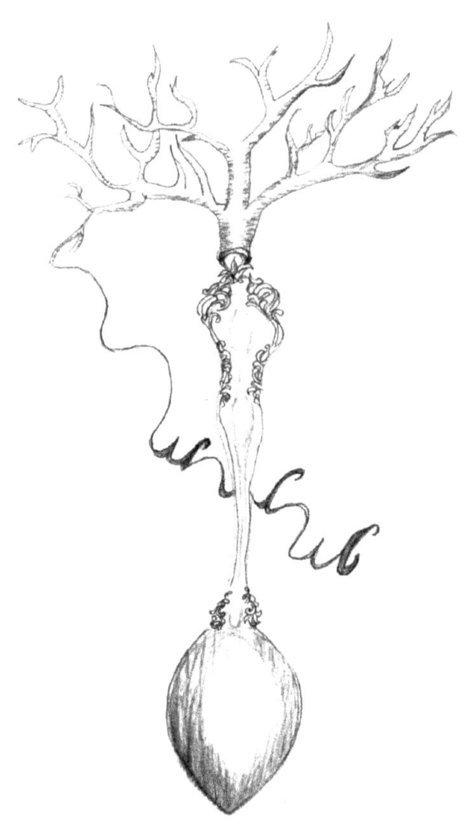

[interlude]

mmm…

thinking about
nutrition that hits your heart
spoon-fed forgiveness

                              delicious

incomparable, right?

splintered leaves won't give up,
as long as they're full

somehow,
undying
your stomach is ever-famished   a leech that rots in soils fertile
pasteurizer

dry seed is decomposed

    somehow,
    you stay starved

[commentary]

My dear,

as you whirl in your metamorphosis
I understand the wind takes its toll
keep looking at you, in the ever-ending ripples of ponds
understand they are age markers
    reflected only,
    they are not stains

you may ruminate here but it is no longer welcome
the grass pushes against your toes, they vocalize their goodbyes
they do want you to stay
    but
isn't growing so weary? an exhaustive eclipse?

there is indeed patience within you

My dear,

I hope you pause to remember the breeze
it may linger and you will touch your chest
to remember
growth
    growing
        ing
           ing

I am growing here
in that mirror, too
stay walking for only in travel you are at your best
sometimes the moments you stay still are meditative
still, the grass comes back
it wraps around a toe or two-

a push-pull

a goodnight, a goodbye

say goodnight to the footprints you scoured over
let them sink into their own path
      as you stamp anew

over-wintered
a plant that is not cold hardy taken indoors or manipulated to keep alive through winter

I have to roll the windows down with you, every time
it could be something in the air but you are also my shocking savior for
picking me up and driving
without question or salutations
there is road and road afront us
we do not stop to feel the flowers you just keep on driving and I keep on trying
to savor familiar breeze

I ask you why this brings me euphoria without a word
you respond by playing that song
the one that transports us into the construction of the home we built
shared space
fire we tended to
you turn up the volume and my ears sigh

please, don't break
please

the road is miraculous because it keeps going
perhaps this was my lithium a subdued conditioning of forgetfulness
a reminder of what lulled me to sleep when I was a baby
rides are motion pictures a movie theater a world-building thrill!!
with you
a spaceship with navigation in full control
these were the times
I consent to this control
yes, I consume this control, let it flow over me

please don't break
let me grow

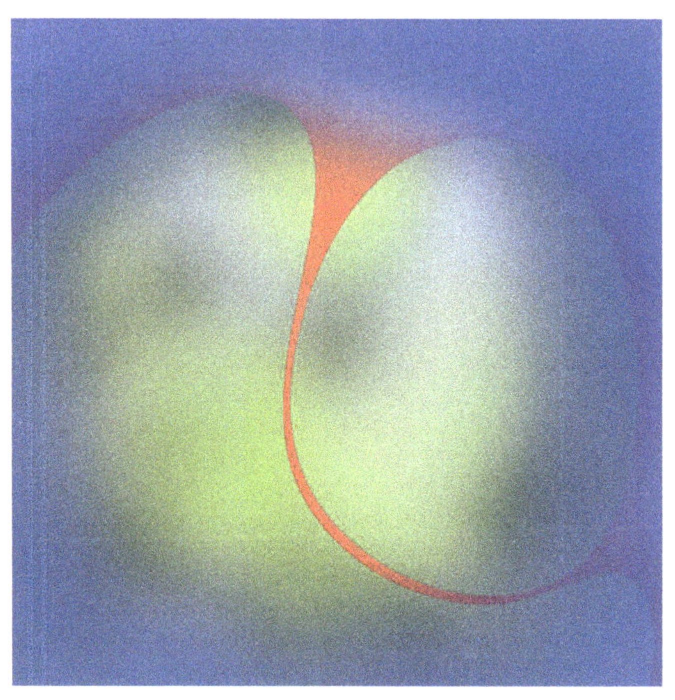

when a seed cannot sprout

it is most difficult to let a dream die you feel the drum of fallen buildings, crushed
galaxies time stops the day it fades and you will feel it in your throat, it swells up in
your eyes the dream   p
                      o
                        u
                           r
                               s
                                   out down your cheek, hits your chin taste
floods as your tongue senses goodbye: the dream, the world, explosions of
foundations, bursting glass windows a crumbling of fragmented sanctuaries
tsunamis out, when the soil is too dry, a goodbye cry

                                             goodbye cry

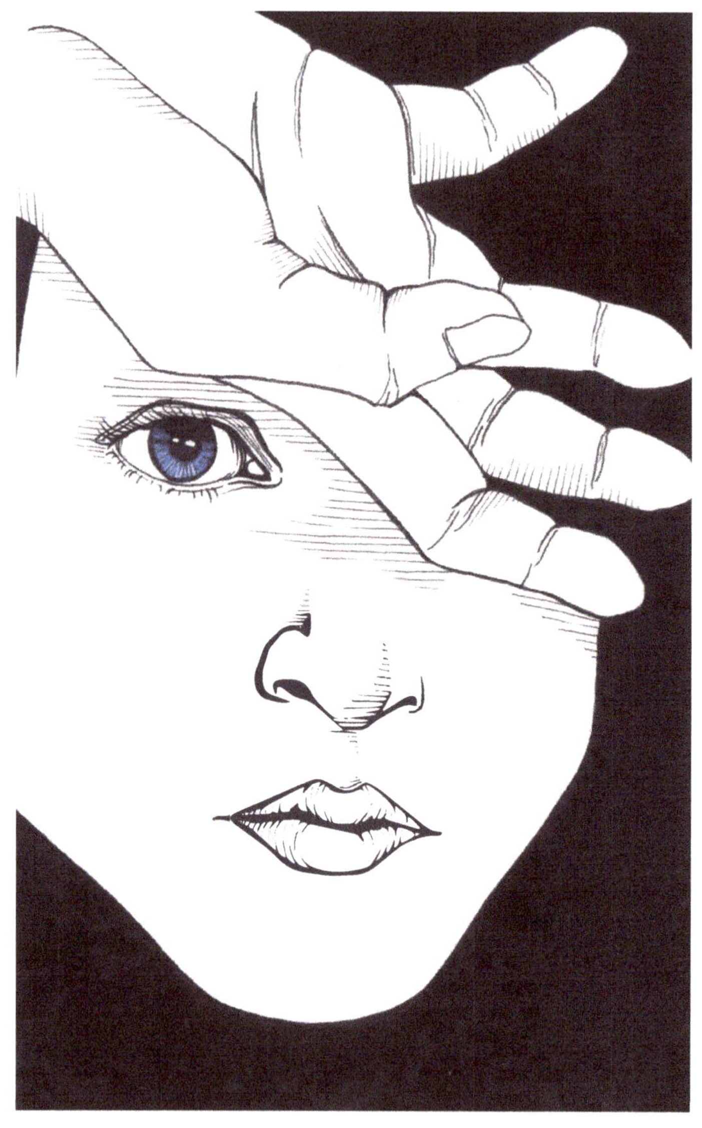

aid

blistering blue underneath
was this the Milky Way you explained?
I'm trying to grasp through your eyes

       so
       sore

I forgot about mine
they're blistering blue underneath
can you see the shade climbing?
a blush flushing up my neck
except
this time it floods in specs

pools of you   internal is tender

is this what your DNA feels like when it expands?

growing pains code blind bruises beneath tissue
pouring rain on my cheeks

little wrists you used to take

              words caused no flinch so your hands spoke
              a dictionary I could not handle
              how lonely this language, how shrunken

              safety tarnished, like the sting of a wax burn

              quick and then…
              cold melt

[commentary]

crystallofolia
frost flowers: an intricate ice formation due to a rupture at the base of a plant in reaction to
freezing temperatures forcefully tearing the epidermis open

my coldest moment was not loud my limbs began to freeze
clocks that cracked patiently
too patient too concerned too caring

this moment is fear: a quiet intuition calling, a reverberated echo as if my whole
body was a canyon every crevice singing to me in dire tones and shrills bones
aching to pull away while standing still

my coldest moment manipulated visibility a tall trunk strong picked away with a
witty ax, leaves plucked with a hidden laugh

                       quiet, no one discusses the quiet

the everlasting poison that brews,
slumbers internal
slow burn erases soft tissues

my coldest moment was frozen stems and trembling leaves
winter without thaw teases hibernation
a spell of snow so quiet strangers smiled as they saw it flurry

snow fell so quick
pillows for my arteries
scrubbing you off heart's skin
raw, turning shades of sanguine
stem is still reaching
peeking through the cold
I stand
shivering blankets warm my wounds
ice painted divots from battle
shifts in seasons
I stand

I confide in the rain…
is it possible to sustain yourself?
provide sun's nutrition
a self-support kit in my cells
where did this water come from?

could this flower provide?
my soil bath
my shower

bloom is still fragile:
I stand

a universal shift
my body: all constellations companionate
exploding suns
the plants in space,
our signs of life
vehemently blue
running wild into cardiac arrest

we become nothing
the stars spangled
our dust
is dust
is air
no longer shared

space swims deep
searching for our deceased

[interlude]

wind speak
   in June

air a haze of violet
sticky and its lungs full
chasing each other
circling
dizzy tumbling down hills
fast smiles eating laughter
some kind of sweet syrup

circling
clutching touch
grasping for warm skin, aura, you

summer evenings are words swimming
fluent and unabashed on my tongue
riding a carrousel of baking winds

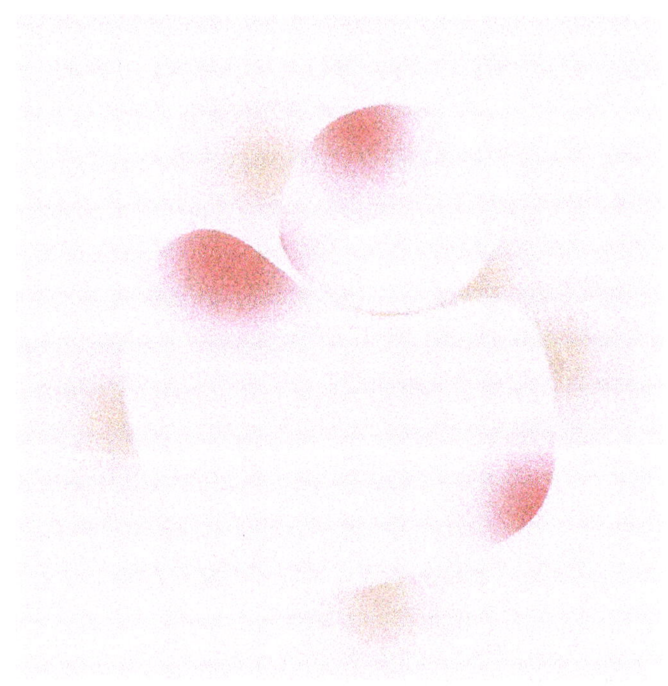

withered

I asked,
water me?   *I was parched*

it was a plea, I wanted to grow   *what harm is a drop?*

on my own, with you
I'd ask when the sun was not speaking
when the moon was not reflected in our river   *the flow was tranquil till roots grew*

I asked, I asked
when petals twisted,
such shrivel
I asked when corners of my stem began to rot

water me? please?
the soil became sand, it was no longer helpful
a blood donor who cannot transfuse
the link was not matched

it poured
so often I crippled dry and forgot to ask what kind of water…

what do *you need?*   *do not stunt your reach*
what are you drinking?

what nutrition is this?
what health?

teething

I've given blood

my rebuke to you is my surgery
I grew the blood back
I flew from the wind in your steps of abandon
laughed in happiness--medicines that pieced together abrasions

a highway without your distraction is a scenic drive
fear clamped around the house key
one of a set of vagaries
foggy musk of the road clouded empathy
there were only threats of a shove against the door
threats of homelessness
threats of shattering wounds further further until they coiled within their own arms

I coiled within my own arms
shaking subsides
breath rains down on muddy pavement
I curve round the bend,
I find fresh patches of grass to burgeon from

[interlude]

self-cleaning
to shed old blooms without human help

I lick the snow off the frostbitten moon
my tongue is stuck there, in some orbital dance
a cosmic function familiar

a rhythm to my being it hums in me the wolves that howled underneath

we are sad because we cannot drink this moon
the way roots seep into its reflection
the way chloroplasts run towards its pull

I sit and clean beneath it all the same,
imagining a ray between my teeth
an embrace with an astronomical body is a comfort I crave
an embrace lightyears ahead

we clean and gleam the energy we can
my muscles twitch to unstick

webbing beneath skin is breakfast for forests a bedding for trees
transportation for unseen

I buried myself

dirt my warm bath, milk for hollowed bones
aches remedied in growth
I leapt into uncertainty for I did not know
who would water
I did not know of sun

dive down, deep into a mind, abyss muddy
my new drink was not pleasant but taste was fair
 hearty,
full and quick to remind there is dirt in our veins
though it may run red or thicken blue

eyelashes coated with soil
ballerina snowflakes too stubborn to melt
earth ate me and spun me out
I died back and I was a seed
a thing often forgotten in a pocket or planted with care
I dug myself there

wind's breath and then I arose
time smiling to reify
imperturbable death continues to pat my land
even-tempered and surprisingly shy

I grab the shovel for life and begin to die again

emersed and native, I only hope for rosettes
day dreaming in a field that feels home
no longer a search or journey to complete
home has grown alongside my silhouette
a terrestrial plant today
stuck on earth without a wisp of air to carry me into orbit
there is peace when my fingers slip
into and out of the meadows that perch beside

elements fostered
elements shared

nodes detach and nuzzle sunlight
finally flying here,
on the ground

goddess Artemis and her gardens
botanist Queens Artemisia I, II
for flavor:
aromatic petals
armor a bitter taste
used to make highly potent spirits
found in teas, herbs, mints,

                repellents

all grow best
unfertilized
in free-draining, sandy soil
in full sun

my *absinthiums, arborescens, jacobaea maritimas*

my medicinal properties
my tradition, therapies, treatment
rituals of
sedative-hypnotic effects
beneficial remedies for reduction of withdrawals

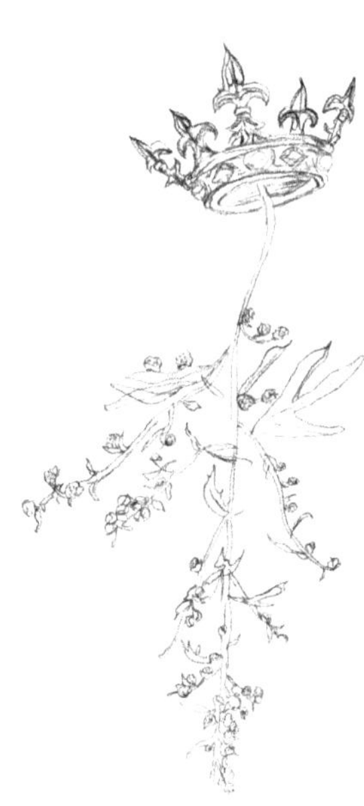

her adaptability,
a cure of fevers in ecosystems of the world

grown alongside various grasses and species of bitter brush
phylogenetic hands
binding activity

Artemisia,
joint with its other flora become enduring habitats
invasive when comfortable
wetlands
        overcompensates,
        due to its ability to grow on poorly enriched soils

artemisinin is at its highest
when harvested at the beginning of flowering

when chemicals fail, physical aid blossoms

my branches are extremely capricious
it's not as composed as you think,
        up there

though I've tied it all together nicely

my mind strings along the clouds, a rope up my tree
a language of flowers
that booklet for gardeners

in this transformation I am a running mammal, gritty jaws and sterile eyes
looking up and over without glancing into peripheral territory
I have never felt stronger, never so broken
no longer a hostage within my own body duality hugs my ribs and grows there

unstoppable and necessary

acceptance of the rush that is everything at once, the staggering does not stop me
it is fuel and hunger

hungry for no fence, for endlessness, hungry for the unbinding the undone

in candlelight your eyes are like mine
I can barely see through the flame but I sketch your gaze
you told me you liked my left eye more than my right
you said it's more inviting
my right knew to keep the sharpener close

changing so much
I feel like myself for the first time

[alternative intro]

spider, returned

careful strangulation twisted my tear
organs confused in this affection
breath caught between two charged hands
passionate removal of roots torn premature
misuse in rooms

you laughed you said you were nervous

I believed until I fell through my mind
it shrunk inside that book you gifted me
a measurement of your growth your newfound adoration in manipulation

of me,
my breaking webs

--

some ask why you return
why from that toxic body of water?

they have not been sand

bee balm

you find it in your skin when you least expect
a homebody you neglect
rejuvenate the ingredient list

put your hands together and open you,
ocean will fill your book
the lines in your palms will shiver in thanks
the water will sink and set

continue the recipe

you've traveled so long your feet ache inward
they tell you to wait and rest, your cocoon is already there
waiting for you by the door, eyes warm, holding all the fruit you need
if your mothers did not tell you
if they did not whisper in you the seeds you now gather,
        alone

continue the recipe:

one fig, open at heart
honey, for glue
time,
to heal

mix and flicker, feel sweaty mist

there is history and it sings underneath
on a humid morning around 5:35am,
sunrise sisters protect and carefully concoct
in still morning they sit and wait for you to climb the mountain
to hike up to release the bonds and binds you've twisted into

drink yourself

[outro]

cotyledon
the first leaves

what does recovery feel like?

   she takes a sip

threatened leaves recede, thorns withdraw under epidermis

eyes wide:
tastes like, feels like…

   terminally budding